You Might Be A Problem Drinker If... Let's Have Another Round!

Also by David L. Anders

You Might Be a Problem Drinker If...

Octogenarians Say the Darndest Things!

20/80 A Love Letter...Sort Of

You Might Be A Problem Drinker If... Let's Have Another Round!

More than 100 Ways to Know What Everyone Else Is Probably Already Thinking

©1999, 2011 David L. Anders
Published in affiliation with David Anders Publishing
House
A subsidiary of
Anders Peachtree City Properties, LLC
PO Box 2422
Peachtree City, GA 30269
E-mail us at: YouMightBe2@AndersUSA.com
Visit our website at: www.AndersUSA.com
Find us on Facebook at David Anders Publishing House

A portion of the earnings from every book sold by
David Anders Publishing House goes to support
underprivileged children in our community.
Find out more at www.AndersUSA.com.

ISBN-10 0615448542
ISBN-13 9780615448541

To Rocky and Lee —
I didn't drink with you more often than I didn't drink with anyone else.
Thanks for the memories!

Introduction, Explanations, Disclaimer, and Apology

In my first book about knowing if you drink too much, *You Might Be A Problem Drinker If ...,* I was met with some criticisms that I might be insensitive to the needs of those who enjoy an occasional libation. Nothing could be farther from the truth, but nevertheless protesters surrounded the international headquarters of David Anders Publishing House, (if one guy with a sign can actually surround anything). Tragedy was narrowly averted when the protestor, who had brought a Molotov cocktail with him, was restrained from drinking the cocktail. You see, some people don't need my help in demonstrating that there really is a problem somewhere.

Others wrote to complain that I seemed to be glorifying alcohol intake, but how does one do that by pointing out the various ways that alcohol consumption might expose one's weaknesses in character and judgment? I certainly haven't been enticed to go out and tie one on after studying the failings of others, and I somehow doubt my readers have either. I feel no temptation to partake in the fruits of the vine, for many different reasons. In fact, several years ago I was asked to teach a Sunday School lesson at my Baptist Church on abstinence from alcohol. In an attempt to shape the message for my listening audience, I came up with a list of the "Top Ten Reasons I Don't Drink", one of which was, "I'm a big enough fool sober". The class offered no protestations in refutation.

"Ah-ha!" you might be saying to yourself, "You are a Baptist, so of course you don't drink." Well, I've been a Baptist long enough to know that's simply not the case. I was told early on in life that about the only difference between many Baptists and Methodists in this regard is that Baptists don't acknowledge each other in the liquor store.

In my formative years I worked as a trombonist in a Dixieland band and attended the University of Georgia. Either of these activities likely deserves its own mention as a potential risk factor for consideration in *You Might Be a Problem Drinker If....* Back then the legal drinking age in Georgia was 18 years of age. During the Viet Nam War the people of Georgia had decided that if you were old enough to kill other people you were old enough to kill yourself.

So it should shock no one reading this book (except perhaps my mother) to hear that I was sometimes around alcohol and encouraged by others to partake in the revelry.

In my first quarter as a freshman at UGA I asked Mary Lynn (that's "Ly-unn" with two syllables in south Georgia), a very attractive Savannah native, out on a date. Not prepared for her answer ("Yes"), I hadn't thought through what we should do on our date. She suggested we could go to a dance club.

This was a new environment for me. Although I had no experience with either, I learned that you went to a dance club to dance and to drink beer. By observation I quickly saw how much easier it seemed to be for others to do the former after having first done a lot of the latter.

Mary Lynn suggested we (meaning I) buy a pitcher of beer. So I reluctantly paid more for a pitcher of beer than I would have paid for a gallon of my preferred beverage, Coke, which actually tasted good. I learned that night that "No Cover" means, "We charge so much for our drinks that you'd have to be crazy to pay this much for a beverage anywhere else, except maybe at a Brave's game."

We took our pitcher and the two six-ounce plastic cups that came with it and sat at our table, which was actually a gigantic wooden spool originally used to store electrical cable. Mary Lynn assumed the duty of barmaid and poured us each a cup of beer. I almost reflexively said, "No thanks," but then realized she expected me to join her for a drink. I hoped she was thirsty. She smiled demurely, cupped her plastic cup in both hands and took a drink from it. I had seen people take bigger sips from mugs of scalding hot coffee. I just stared at my cup and wondered what to do next.

I had spent much of that week fretting about what intelligent conversation I could come up with and what I was going to say to this intimidatingly beautiful belle, but I needn't have worried. I learned that the music in a dance club is played so loudly that all conversation is virtually impossible unless one is an experienced lip reader. This is certainly by design since the only way these clubs make money is to sell drinks — they don't want patrons wasting time talking. Instead dancing, fast and furious, is encouraged since such physical activity is certain to create thirst, which thus generates profits for the club owner. The peanuts are free for the same reason — they make you thirsty, so you'll drink more beer. Being on a limited budget, I was glad to try to make up my losses on the night thus far by gorging on peanuts.

Not yet thirsty enough to further contemplate how much of the pitcher she thought it was my responsibility to empty, I resigned myself to the reality that the only other thing left to do was to ask her to dance. I had been to lots of dances, but in high school you could go to a dance and stand around all night, never having to actually dance. I couldn't quite envision that being an option here, so I gesticulated that we should go dance. We made our way out to the crowded floor. Not knowing what to do with my cup of beer, I took mine with me, but left the pitcher hoping that someone would steal it while we were gone. Or maybe a waitress would clear our table in our absence.

As long as you are not very easily embarrassed, it's not hard to be a good dancer, or at least to perceive yourself as being a good dancer, at a crowded dance club. I quickly learned from imitating those around me and started dancing, all the while trying not to spill my still-full cup of beer. But after a few sloshes I realized that the carpeted floor nicely absorbed spills, and in the crowded noisy dark room my spills went unnoticed. I felt like a hypocrite as I periodically lifted my cup to my lips without drinking, and then when my date wasn't looking sloshed even more of my beer to the ground.

And so went my evening. When all was said and done, Mary Lynn had taken about three sips from her cup, although I'm not sure the level of her drink ever went down. I slowly emptied most of that entire pitcher onto the floor one cup at a time while we danced or when she went to the ladies' room.

We walked home, finally able to talk. We talked about what a great time we had. That was the last great time we had together.

That same year some well-intentioned friends encouraged me to "learn" how to drink. They considered themselves authorities on fine adult beverages, and felt a sophisticated gentleman should cultivate a palate for the tasty concoctions they described. One night four of us went to a jazz club to hear some of

Atlanta's finest Dixieland musicians: Sammy Duncan on trumpet, Spider Ridgeway on the drums, Herman "Shirt" Foretich on clarinet, and the man I wanted to hear on trombone, Charlie Bornemann. I had heard that Charlie could hit a double high B-flat, a full octave higher than notes I usually felt comfortable playing on my trombone when on-stage.

As we entered the club I was surprised that we didn't have to buy a ticket or pay to get in; there was no "cover charge". What I didn't expect was that there was a "two drink minimum". I learned that night that a "minimum" usually means, "We've got entertainment worth paying for, however you're too cheap or too unsophisticated to know the value of the talent. But we know you'll buy drinks at any cost, so we'll nail you on the price of the drinks." Or something like that.

I thought I would beat the system by ordering two Cokes, but my friend warned me that soft drinks would cost the same as mixed drinks, and both would be served in six-ounce glasses. That made me mad. I'd rather pay an entertainment fee and be able to get free refills on a large Coke. Who made these rules?

So my friend advised that I start off my voyage by ordering a "sloe gin fizz". He explained that while this drink had alcohol in it, I wouldn't taste the alcohol. It seemed to me that seemed to defeat the purpose of drinking — wouldn't it be cheaper to just leave the alcohol out altogether? — but I was so angry about the cost of beverages in this establishment that I was letting him steer me. Not that I had any intention of drinking the alcohol, but I sure wasn't going to let them rip me off.

To save time, the waitress took our orders for both drinks — I ordered two sloe gin fizzes — and collected our money - $2.50 per drink — before the music started. I think she knew no one in their right mind was otherwise going to pay for those drinks, and we looked like the kind of guys that couldn't be trusted. What right-minded teenaged boys in the 1970's were going to Dixieland clubs?

She delivered our drinks, and the show still hadn't started. I offered to sell my drinks for a dollar each to the other guys at my table. I was surprised there were no takers. These men of the world who were interested in educating me in fine spirits, who had spent so much of the evening to that point talking about what made a fine beverage, describing the subtle flavors and delicious tastes which awaited me, had no interest in this truly delectable bargain — 60% off retail price. Heck, if this had been Coke, I could have downed six or seven of these sissy-sized glasses before the show started. But they didn't seem much more interested in drinking their drinks than Mary Lynn had been in her beer. It took them the entire 90 minute set to finish all or most of their drinks, and mine slowly warmed to room temperature, untouched even when the sale price was reduced to 100% off.

Through observation I did learn a good bit about drinking that night, and Charlie hit the double B-flat on *Basin Street Blues*, and I ate my weight in peanuts, so all-in-all I had a good time. In fact, it would have been a perfect night if I hadn't felt so exploited by the drink policy.

As my freshman year at UGA progressed I had many more opportunities to drink or not to drink, and to observe those who did. I wasn't self-conscious about being a non-drinker in a drinking world, but became amused by how it seemed to irritate some folks that I didn't endorse their choices by imbibing. I was chagrinned to observe how interested people at parties are in knowing what other people are drinking. Go to a party in college and hold a cup of water. People will come up and ask, "What are you drinking?" Why should they care? When I would respond, "Water," sometimes the questioner would murmur a curse, as though it were unfair that I could feel comfortable in going to a party and not drinking. Or perhaps they just didn't like my taste in leisure suits.

Or their response might reveal an apparent obligation to proselytize me to the temple of Bachus. "Here, try this," they would say, offering to let me have their drink. I would politely decline, then they'd go off and slosh their drink on the carpet. Sometimes, the questioner replied, "Yeah, I think I'll switch over now, too," as if they felt concerned about their drinking. The truth be told, I think the drinkers spent a lot more time worrying about their drinking or my not drinking than I did, but who knows? In college, you seek solutions to your insecurities.

By the beginning of my sophomore year at UGA I had no insecurities about not drinking. I was amazed how much time, money and conversation were wasted arguing about who could drink how much of what. One night two of my roommates were arguing about who could drink a little six-ounce bottle of beer called a "pony" the fastest. I'm not kidding when I'm telling you these two grown men spent over 15 minutes bickering and bragging over who could chug the bottle. After 15 minutes, I felt moved by the muse of comedy. I walked over, picked up the bottle, chugged the entire contents, and left the room without saying a word. They both realized that if I could do that, it really was no big deal, and not a further word was said about that topic the rest of the evening. I was too proud, of course, to let them know I immediately went down to the bathroom and threw up. A comedian has to be willing to suffer for his art.

I remained fairly non-judgmental about alcohol. In fact, a few years later when one of the aforementioned roommates announced his engagement, I thought I'd crossover with an olive branch, a ringing endorsement of his happiness and life's choices and buy him something he might not buy himself, a high-quality bottle of vintage champagne. I went to the local convenience store, ready to spare no expense, as long as it cost me less than $8. Not really knowing what to buy, I grabbed the first bottle that I saw, pleased to see just how much within my budget I had managed to stay, and headed for the check-out line. To my surprise, my former Minister of Music was in line just before me. I violated protocol and said "hello" to him. He was too polite to ask about the single item I had to purchase.

Ultimately, the only thing that really appealed to me about drinking was all the funny things that seemed to happen where alcohol was involved, and I realized I didn't have to spend a lot of money to have fun — I just had to be present. I rapidly became the designated driver and usually wound up having the most fun of anyone present, or at least I could remember having the most fun. I had many opportunities to serve as designated driver for my musician friends and other co-workers as we spent summers together as a band. Not that doing so was totally risk free.

One late night in Pittsburg with a car full of musicians I was pulled over by a policeman. He had seen my ancient Ford Maverick swerve over the center line as I made a wide-sweeping right hand turn, the only kind of right hand turn you could make in that car because the suspension was so bad. He pulled me over and came up to the side of the car. I'm certain the other three guys in the car were breathing a collective sigh of relief that they were not driving. That collective sigh would have affected the ambient air levels inside the car such that they would have lit up a breathalyzer. As I rolled down my window, his first question after receiving my license was, "Mr. Anders, have you been drinking tonight?"

This particular question struck my passengers as most amusing, and their unsuccessfully stifled eructations of laughter, the irony of the question, along with the early morning two-o'clock hour made me giggle also. Not smart. The officer spent the next fifteen minutes trying to impress me with his skills in administering the various roadside tests used to identify the impaired driver. Ultimately, he was convinced that I was more of a help than a hindrance, but only after I had undergone a more thorough neuropsychiatric examination than most NASA applicants. The poorly suppressed snickering coming from the car did nothing to improve his humor.

Wow — I didn't really plan to write so much before starting on with the main portion of the book. But you know how it is with alcohol, or sometimes just talking about alcohol. It really seems to make some folks spill their guts, literally or figuratively. And now, so have I.

So you can see, despite what the critics and protestors have claimed, I didn't write the first volume of *You Might Be A Problem Drinker If...* because of some moralizing high-mindedness I had with a holier-than-thou attitude. You can clearly see I don't drink because I'm too cheap, I throw up, and I'm a big enough fool already.

Now that we've gotten that out of the way, *Let's Have Another Round!*

You Might Be A Problem Drinker If...

On a cold winter morning the smell of your breath travels further than its vapor.

You Might Be A Problem Drinker If...

You have a piece of the goalpost from the 2003 Rose Bowl.

You Might Be A Problem Drinker If...

Your year doesn't actually begin until
January 2nd.

You Might Be A Problem Drinker If...

The last time you were at McDonald's you ordered a bucket of chicken.

You Might Be A Problem Drinker If...

You once punched out a pay phone.

You Might Be A Problem Drinker If...

You have ever had your first and last meal of the same day at a Waffle House.

You Might Be A Problem Drinker If...

The floor of your workshop is sticky.

You Might Be A Problem Drinker If...

Someone once started CPR on you without first checking for a pulse.

You Might Be A Problem Drinker If...

You've tried to change channels on your television set using your cellular phone.

You Might Be A Problem Drinker If...

You once made a pilgrimage to Lynchburg, Tennessee.

You Might Be A Problem Drinker If...

At a baseball game you once stood and sang a rousing rendition of "The Star Spangled Banner"... during the seventh inning stretch.

You Might Be A Problem Drinker If...

The replacement value of the alcoholic beverages at your home exceeds the coverage provided by your homeowner's insurance policy.

You Might Be A Problem Drinker If...

You dozed off during your wedding ceremony

You Might Be A Problem Drinker If...

You have ruined a silk tie by wearing it in the shower.

You Might Be A Problem Drinker If...

Sponsors of a local chug-a-lug contest declare you ineligible to compete as an amateur.

You Might Be A Problem Drinker If...

You accidentally spill your drink on the carpet and it removes a seven-year-old stain.

You Might Be A Problem Drinker If...

You have ever bowled a perfect "0" game.

You Might Be A Problem Drinker If...

You paid retail for this book.

You Might Be A Problem Drinker If...

You think Beethoven's Fifth was a type of beverage.

You Might Be A Problem Drinker If...

You take an aptitude test for career guidance and are advised to become a politician.

You Might Be A Problem Drinker If...

You enjoy napping on asphalt.

You Might Be A Problem Drinker If...

You keep a one gallon jug at your bedside for the sake of convenience.

You Might Be A Problem Drinker If...

You missed Sunday morning church because you never heard the bartender give last call.

You Might Be A Problem Drinker If...

When you decided to "get on the wagon", it was pulled by Clydesdales.

You Might Be A Problem Drinker If...

After listening to your comments a talk-radio host asks, "When did you have your stroke?"

You Might Be A Problem Drinker If...

You have ever broken into a public swimming pool after midnight to go skinny-dipping.

You Might Be A Problem Drinker If...

You pride yourself on your ability to open a bottle of beer with your teeth.

You Might Be A Problem Drinker If...

You refer to death as "the ultimate last call".

You Might Be A Problem Drinker If...

You wake up with a tattoo.

You Might Be A Problem Drinker If...

Your chest X-ray report includes a description of an incidental finding of scattered buckshot.

You Might Be A Problem Drinker If...

Your key ring has a bottle opener on it.

You Might Be A Problem Drinker If...

You know for a fact that your door key does not fit your neighbor's front door.

You Might Be A Problem Drinker If...

You have ever been swimming with the Polar Bear Club.

You Might Be A Problem Drinker If...

The first button on your phone's speed dial is a package store.

You Might Be A Problem Drinker If...

You have ever used a pool cue as a weapon.

You Might Be A Problem Drinker If...

You have ever had to shave your head because you lost a bet.

You Might Be A Problem Drinker If...

The budget for your annual office party
includes your bail bond expense.

You Might Be A Problem Drinker If...

You have ever inspired a group of people to speak in tongues, and you're not Pentecostal.

You Might Be A Problem Drinker If...

The sign on the wall in your department reads: "000 injury free days in the last 365 days", and you're the only one in your department who has been hurt.

You Might Be A Problem Drinker If...

You have stuffed a goose before killing it.

You Might Be A Problem Drinker If...

Your dog drinks beer.

You Might Be A Problem Drinker If...

You let your dog drink beer.

You Might Be A Problem Drinker If...

You keep a six-pack in your neighbor's refrigerator.

You Might Be A Problem Drinker If...

You called eight or more friends at 3:00 AM to tell them you had the winning Lotto ticket, only to realize the next day that the "7" was actually a "1".

You Might Be A Problem Drinker If...

The word "proof" appears on both your baby pictures and your baby bottle.

You Might Be A Problem Drinker If...

You refer to corn alcohol as "an
alternative fuel source".

You Might Be A Problem Drinker If...

On your driver's license your eye color is listed as "red".

You Might Be A Problem Drinker If...

You drive across county lines on Sunday
to buy beer.

~ # 48 ~

You Might Be A Problem Drinker If...

At one point in time it seemed reasonable to put the Fudgesicle in your trousers' pocket.

You Might Be A Problem Drinker If...

You know what antifreeze tastes like.

You Might Be A Problem Drinker If...

Your invitation to your niece's wedding and rehearsal dinner were lost in the mail.

You Might Be A Problem Drinker If...

You re-enlisted.

You Might Be A Problem Drinker If...

The shoes you are wearing right now don't match.

You Might Be A Problem Drinker If...

Your wife tells you her mother "was right all along".

You Might Be A Problem Drinker If...

You arrive at work a few minutes early so you can iron your tie in the fax machine.

You Might Be A Problem Drinker If...

You break seven of the Ten Commandments in one 24-hour period of time.

You Might Be A Problem Drinker If...

You miss the beer commercials whenever you watch HBO.

You Might Be A Problem Drinker If...

You have ever eaten a live roach.

You Might Be A Problem Drinker If...

You have an Ed McMahon lunch box.

You Might Be A Problem Drinker If...

At your friend's funeral you are asked to
be "Pall Mall Bearer".

You Might Be A Problem Drinker If...

You couldn't stop giggling at your roommate's wedding.

You Might Be A Problem Drinker If...

You see more than one of the same thing at the same time.

You Might Be A Problem Drinker If...

You see more than one of the same thing at the same time.

You Might Be A Problem Drinker If...

You decide to add a bonus room, building it from memory based on previous episodes of "This Old House".

~ # 64 ~

You Might Be A Problem Drinker If...

After drinking your blood a vampire begins singing "Show Me The Way To Go Home".

You Might Be A Problem Drinker If...

Your wife is on the phone with the neighbor telling her, "Well, what I *hope* he's doing is spraying *insecticide* on the ant hills".

You Might Be A Problem Drinker If...

To demonstrate you have conquered your fear of flying you attempt to board the Atlanta to Los Angeles flight with a boarding pass from Greyhound.

You Might Be A Problem Drinker If...

You refer to tonic water as "dilutant".

You Might Be A Problem Drinker If...

You have ever shaved a cat.

You Might Be A Problem Drinker If...

You have ever told someone you loved them, hoping they would give you their beer.

~ # 70 ~

You Might Be A Problem Drinker If...

You once woke up in a pool of vomit...
and weren't certain it was your own.

You Might Be A Problem Drinker If...

You have ever sent out photocopies of an apology.

You Might Be A
Problem Drinker If...

You make it to the sports section before
you realize the newspaper you're reading
is three years old.

You Might Be A Problem Drinker If...

The photographer at your brother's wedding charges an extra fee to PhotoShop the group picture so it looks like you're standing up.

You Might Be A Problem Drinker If...

You were disappointed to learn that "Meet the Press" was not a television documentary on wine making.

You Might Be A Problem Drinker If...

You suffer a flash burn to the face after accidentally sneezing on the barbecue grill.

You Might Be A Problem Drinker If...

Your bicycle has ever been impounded.

You Might Be A Problem Drinker If...

You are more likely to invoke the name of Jesus Christ on a Saturday night than a Sunday morning.

~ # 78 ~

You Might Be A Problem Drinker If...

You can quote the alcoholic content of artificial vanilla flavoring, Nyquil, and Listerine.

You Might Be A Problem Drinker If...

Santa leaves his empties by your tree every year.

You Might Be A Problem Drinker If...

The police department has its own unique special signal code response number for anything involving you.

You Might Be A Problem Drinker If...

You hit on your mother-in-law last New Year's Eve.

You Might Be A Problem Drinker If...

You envy a dog's liberty to use any available tree.

You Might Be A Problem Drinker If...

Your son "forgot" to tell you that yesterday was "Bring Your Dad to School Day".

You Might Be A Problem Drinker If...

You are immune to Antabuse.

You Might Be A Problem Drinker If...

Around your country club you are known as "The Club Pro of the 19th Hole".

You Might Be A Problem Drinker If...

You complained that alcoholic drinks were not a prize in the "You Might Be a Problem Drinker If..." contest. (Shameless plug — See back of book for contest details.)

~ # 87 ~

You Might Be A Problem Drinker If...

Your dog sleeps with one eye opened.

You Might Be A Problem Drinker If...

You assume your friends gave you an Emerson Boozer jersey because in your day you were such a talented running back.

You Might Be A Problem Drinker If...

You reasoned that since a bicycle is essentially two inner tubes, you would be able to ride it across the lake.

You Might Be A Problem Drinker If...

You feel comfortable anywhere in the world since you know how to ask for "bier", "birrë", "يرة بـ", "զաբեջուր", "pivə", "garagardoa", "пива", "啤酒", "pivo", "øl", "õlu", "la bière", "ლუდი", "μπίρα", "בירה", "बियर", "ビール", "alus", "piwo", "пиво", and "cwrw", to name but a few.

You Might Be A Problem Drinker If...

When your swim suit starts to slip down while you demonstrate your water-skiing skills, pride makes you refuse to let go of the rope, foolishness makes you refuse to let go of your beer.

You Might Be A Problem Drinker If...

You don't understand why all your friends keep saying, "You've got to read this book!"

You Might Be A Problem Drinker If...

One of your softball traditions is the "Seventh Inning Retch".

You Might Be A Problem Drinker If...

Warning signs always seem to be meant for other people.

You Might Be A Problem Drinker If...

After performing your interpretation of the "Moonwalk" you are arrested for indecent exposure.

You Might Be A Problem Drinker If...

Whenever you drink grape juice you comment, "It's not ready yet."

You Might Be A Problem Drinker If...

You forgot why you bought this book.

~ # 98 ~

You Might Be A Problem Drinker If...

Every day you spend $7 on cigarrettes and $8 on alcohol, but you scream at your doctor that you can't possibly afford the blood pressure pills he prescribed that cost $2 per day.

You Might Be A Problem Drinker If...

You once spent an entire October afternoon planting corn.

You Might Be A Problem Drinker If...

The recipe for your favorite mixed drink begins, "Pour the contents of one bottle of rum..."

You Might Be A Problem Drinker If...

You like the idea of performing in an armpit choir.

You Might Be A Problem Drinker If...

Your socks smell like cigarette smoke.

You Might Be A Problem Drinker If...

While watching videos of your cousin's wedding, you ask, "Who was that stumbling drunk?" just before recognizing the bottom of your shoes.

Announcing The "You Might Be A Problem Drinker If..." Writer's Contest

You could be the next great American writer! We need your help in writing our next book in the series "You Might Be A Problem Drinker If..."!

Just go online at *www.AndersUSA.com* and send us your original quip, observation, advice, or otherwise humorous thought to complete the sentence, "You Might Be A Problem Drinker If...", and you might be selected as a winner. Winners' entries will be published in the forthcoming *You Might Be A Problem Drinker If... Time For Some Home Brew!* and every winner will receive a free copy of the book, suitable for framing. (Meaning your friends might use your participation as evidence against you at work.) Enter as often as you like as long as you are at least 21 years of age, but only one prize per person, no matter how many times we slander you by publishing your entries.

So get thinking now and join in on the fun. Suffering from writer's block? You may want to read the first book in the series for ideas: *You Might Be A Problem Drinker If...* or re-read this book again. Not that either of these books will inspire greatness, but haven't we all been able to learn from a bad example?

Our lawyers want us to be certain to remind you to read the contest rules before entering. Just sayin'. So we've posted them online at *www.AndersUSA.com* or you can download a copy for your collection if you are really bored.

About the Author

Dr. David L. Anders lives in Peachtree City, GA where he practices Internal Medicine and Geriatrics. He and his wife, Kenya, have five children: Rebekah, Lloyd, Luke, Rachel, and Lincoln.

David welcomes your comments to him by e-mail c/o his Executive Assistant at:

Attn: Fred Carey, Executive Assistant
YouMightBe2@AndersUSA.com

Or write via U.S. mail at:
David Anders Publishing House
PO Box 2422
Peachtree City, GA 30269

Drop by our website at
www.AndersUSA.com

Find us on Facebook at
David Anders Publishing House

David Anders Publishing House — a Writer's Studio® was established to provide new authors assistance with access to the world of professional publication. As a publisher of quality writings we hope to be adding continuously to our studio of writers and the list of their fine works.

If you have a friend who is trying to get a book published, tell him or her about us — or maybe you are ready to take that step yourself. Visit our website and bookstore at www.AndersUSA.com.

Books we are proud to be featuring currently include:

20/80 A Love Letter...Sort Of
by David L. Anders

This fictional romantic comedy is a story of humor, romance, wisdom and foolishness.

David Patson is a Pre-Med student at the University of Georgia who awakens carefree on his 20th birthday, May 25, 1977, then meets three uninvited strangers who crash his party and take him on what can only be described as the journey of a lifetime.

Octogenarians Say the Darndest Things
by David L. Anders with Rebekah Yates Anders

Life doesn't begin at 80, but it doesn't have to end there either. This mother-son team of physicians with over 75 years of patient care experience recalls the humor, wisdom, pathos and surprises revealed while caring for this remarkable group of people.

The Silver Bell
by Rebekah Yates Anders
with illustrations by Rachel Elizabeth Anders

In this short story for children and adults, a young boy demonstrates caring and another view of the love of Christmas is revealed.

Signs of The Times
by Kenya Houghton Anders

By combining familiar traffic signs with valuable scripture verses, students of any age will find learning Bible verses easier and more enjoyable.

You Might Be a Problem Drinker If...
by David L. Anders
Hilarious and yet insightful, more than 100 ways to know if maybe it's time to cut down on the drinking (or increase your life insurance coverage!).

www.ingramcontent.com/pod-product-compliance
Lightning Source LLC
Chambersburg PA
CBHW060942040426
42445CB00011B/963